This book is dedicated to my mother, Leslie Kim Berry and my grandmother, Eleanor Barbara Berry. Cheers to plans A-Z.

About the Author

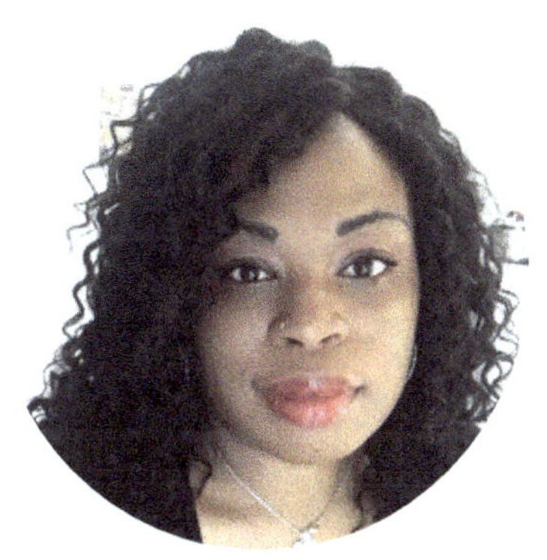

ELLIE B.

Ellie B. is an American educator and self-taught artist currently residing in China.

Ellie B. Gallery is a collection of original, thought-provoking, and emotionally expressive artwork created by Ellie B. The company was formed in 2022 as a living tribute to Ellie B.'s grandmother, Eleanor Barbara Berry.

This journal is for anyone who needs a space to feel cherished, empowered, and productive. All the paintings in this journal are the original works of Ellie B.

Enjoy!

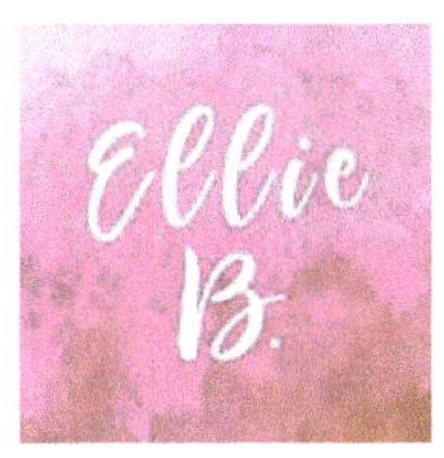

WWW.ELLIEB.GALLERY

How to Use This Book

Since you bought it, you can do anything you want with this journal!

Here are a few options:

- Sketch
- Write a poem
- Free write/journal
- Use the affirmations from the word clouds on each page for inspiration

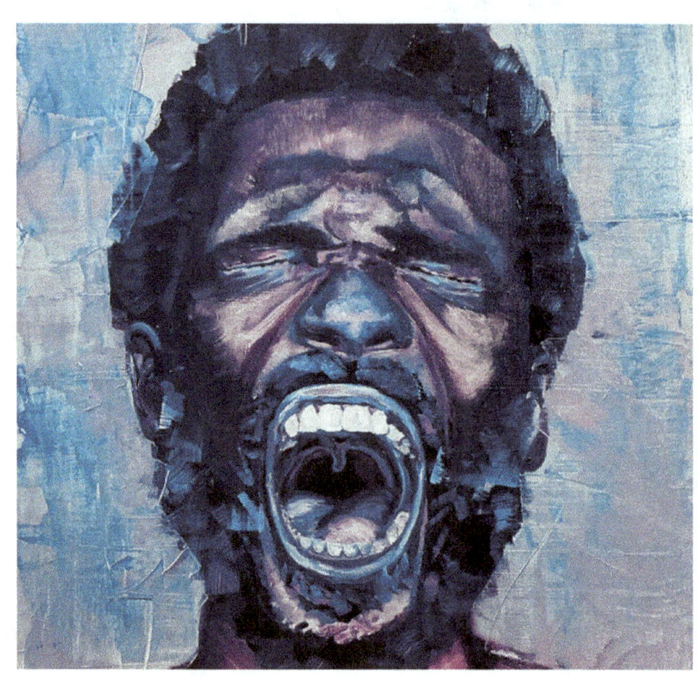

"AGONY", OIL ON CANVAS, 2021

Check out my cinquain

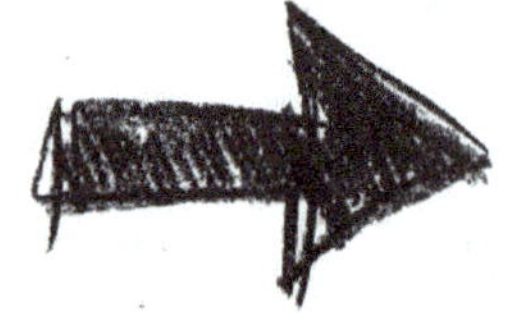

A loss
Bitter, painful
Crying, screaming, thinking
Searching for answers in the dark
Empty.

A cinquain poem consists of five lines:

Line 1: the topic (2 syllables)
Line 2: adjectives(4 syllables)
Line 3: -ing verbs (6 syllables)
Line 4: a phrase that describes the emotions of the topic (8 syllables)
Line 5: adjective about line 1 (2 syllables)

Try it!

Themes and Prompts

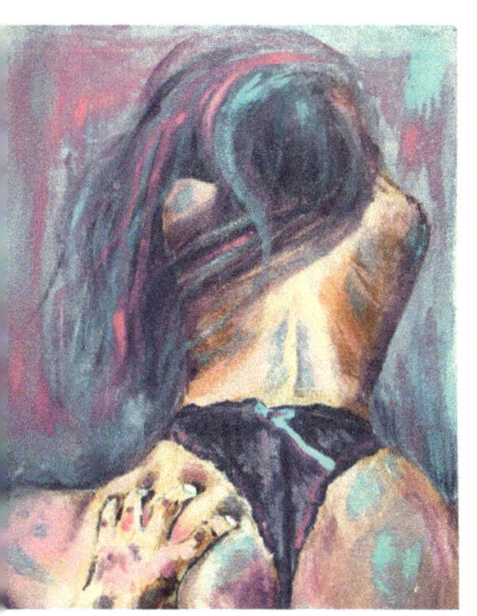

e Grab", 2020, oil on canvas

What words come to mind when you look at these paintings? Use those words to create something magical.

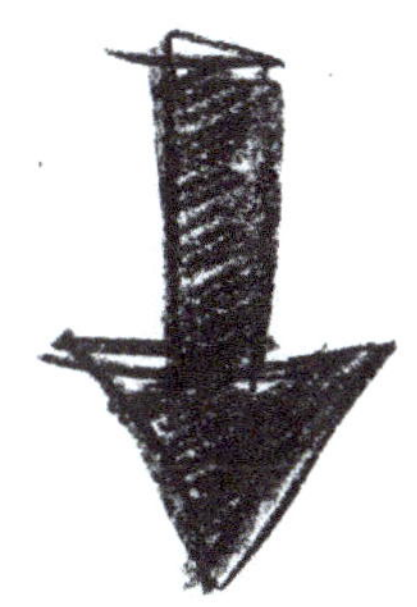

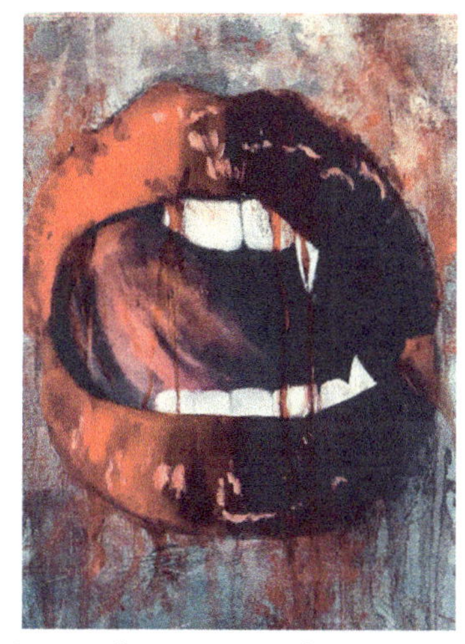

"Thirsty", 2020, oil on canvas

Need more ideas? Jot down your thoughts here and get ready to create!

Humans
Heart
Technology
Repetition
Fears
tasy/Dreams
Love
Soul
Balance
Nature
Conflict
Identity
Time

Assertive

Authentic

Ambitious

Adventurous

Breathtaking

Badass

Beautiful

Brave

Brilliant

Creative

Classy

Courageous

Charismatic

Celebrated

Capable

Confident

Daring

Different

Divine

Diverse

Educated

Exotic

Experienced

Fashionable

Fierce

Gentle

Genuine

Gifted

Glamorous

Grounded

Hot

Honest

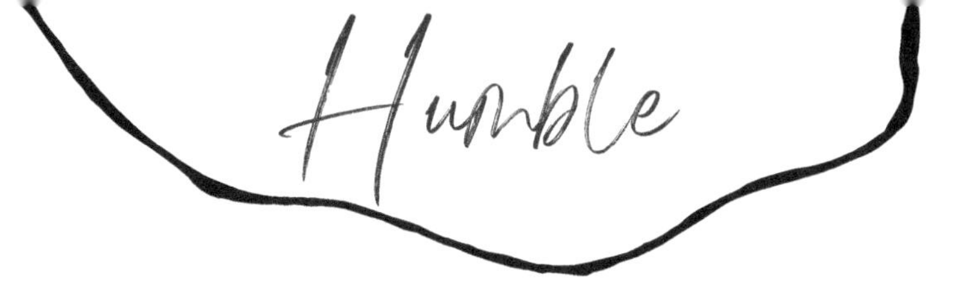
Humble

Independent

Innovative

Intoxicating

Invincible

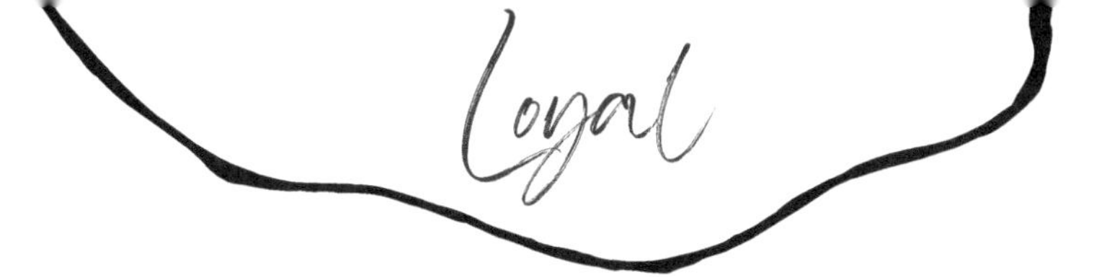
Loyal

Mesmerizing

Mindful

Motivated

Phenomenal

Sensual

Sexy

Stunning

Unique

Unbreakable

Visionary

Worthy

You

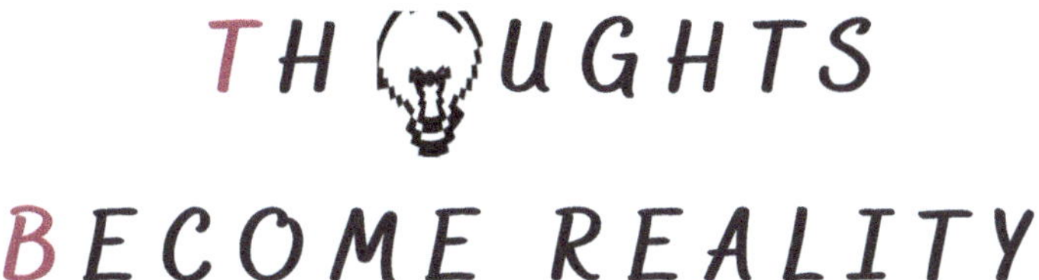

THOUGHTS BECOME REALITY

Using the space below, say goodbye to the person you once were. Welcome a promising future.

www.ingramcontent.com/pod-product-compliance
Lightning Source LLC
LaVergne TN
LVHW061251100826
845148LV00008B/1094

9798986000411